Words I Never Said

Shrest Sharma

BookLeaf Publishing

India | USA | UK

Dedication

To my **Mom, Dad, and Sister**—your love, sacrifices, and unwavering support have been the foundation of my dreams.

To my **teachers**, who have enlightened my path with knowledge, wisdom, and guidance. Your lessons extend beyond books and have shaped my understanding of the world.

To my **family**, whose encouragement has been my strength, and to all my friends and mentors who have inspired me along the way.

This book is a tribute to all of you—thank you for being a part of my journey.

Preface

Writing this book has been a journey filled with learning, challenges, and moments of inspiration. The idea behind these pages was born from a deep curiosity and a desire to explore, understand, and share knowledge. Whether you are a student, a professional, or simply someone eager to learn, I hope this book provides value, sparks curiosity, and encourages new perspectives.

As I put my thoughts into words, I realized that this book is not just a collection of ideas but a reflection of my experiences, my passion for learning, and the support of the incredible people in my life. Every chapter represents a piece of my journey, and I am grateful for the opportunity to share it with you.

I sincerely hope this book adds something meaningful to your path, just as writing it has added to mine.

Acknowledgements

No journey is ever undertaken alone, and this book is no exception.

First and foremost, I express my deepest gratitude to my **Mom and Dad**, whose constant encouragement, sacrifices, and love have been the foundation of my aspirations. To my **Sister**, my lifelong companion, and my entire **family**, thank you for being my source of motivation and strength.

To my **teachers, mentors, and friends**, who have guided me, challenged me, and enriched my journey—your insights and support have been invaluable.

Lastly, I am grateful to **everyone who believed in me**, to the experiences that shaped me, and to the moments of struggle that taught me resilience. This book is a testament to all the lessons I've learned and the incredible people who have walked this path with me. Thank you!

1. The Whisper of Nature

In the quiet of the forest, where the whispering leaves
Speak of truths as ancient as time, and secrets it weaves,
There lies wisdom, deep in the roots and the air,
A lesson in letting go, in the act of true care.

The river flows onward, never asking the stones
To remain in its path, nor the fish in their zones.
It knows its direction, yet carries what may,
And those who must part, it allows them their way.

The wind through the branches, a gentle caress,
Does not hold the leaves, though it loves them no less.
In autumn they scatter, in a dance of farewell,
Yet the tree stands undeterred, for it knows them well.

Birds take to the sky, on a migratory flight,
Never chained to the branches, nor held by the night.
Their journey is theirs, and the sky does not bind,
For freedom is written in the vast open mind.

Mountains stand witness, to the fleeting of clouds,
To the coming and going, of mists and of shrouds.
Unmoved by their passing, serene in their height,
They teach us patience, of holding not tight.

So learn from the forest, the river, the breeze,
From mountains and birds, and the whispering trees.
In the heart of true love, there's a space to be free,
To let those we cherish find where they must be.

For those meant to stay will return in due course,
And those who must leave, find their path, their own
source.
In the end, all returns to the circle, the way,
That nature ordains, in its wisdom, we pray.

2. Dappled Illusions

Sunlight strains through leafy lace,
dappled beams upon my face.
I lift my eyes, but see no sign,
of empathy, or tickers entwined.

The world spins on in careless rhyme,
oblivious to passing time.
My silent pleas unheard, unseen,
lost whispers in a verdant scene.

Beneath the boughs, a hidden tear,
A secret hurt, a whispered fear.
Are these companions just a show?
A painted warmth with nowhere to go?

Kind words exchanged, like empty chimes,
Ringing hollow through these bleak times.
Longing for solace, a hand to hold,
But facades crumble, leaving me cold.

Is this the price of hearts that hide?
Yearning for connection, nowhere to confide?
The sun dips low, paints the leaves with fire,
As shadows lengthen, and hope seems to tire.

Masks they wear, with smiles so bright,
But shadows lurk in hidden night.
Their words like whispers, sweet and coy,
But hold no warmth, no real alloy.

3. The Weight of Silence

I've been the one who holds the strings,
Who weaves the bonds and ties the rings,
But silence falls when it's my turn,
To ask for the love I also yearn.

I've watched them come, I've watched them go,
Their eyes alight with someone's glow.
I stayed behind, I patched the seams,
Holding together forgotten dreams.

And when another whispers near,
With glazing words I cannot hear,
They pull away, like autumn leaves,
And I am left where silence cleaves.

They run to promises of bliss,
To hands that take but never miss,
The cracks they leave in hearts they've known,
Now scattered seeds, unborn, unsown.

I've asked myself in quieter nights,
Why must I always mend the fights?
Why must I always bridge the gap,
When no one waits to unleash the trap?

But here's the truth I've come to learn:
Some fire flickers, some must burn.
Not all who leave are meant to stay,
Not all who care can find the way.

So let them go, if they must choose,
There's nothing more that you can lose.
In stillness, find the strength to stand,
For those who stay will hold your hand.

Disrespect will come and go,
But peace is something, you can grow.
Stay calm, stay true, and you will find,
That those who leave, were truly kind.

4. The Healer's Need

They call you strong, the healer's heart,
You mend each soul that's torn apart.
With hands that soothe and words that mend,
You're the balm on wounds that never end.

But who heals you, dear healer wise,
When sorrow clouds your steady eyes?
When your strength, a thread so finely spun,
Feels stretched, unraveling one by one?

People drift like autumn leaves,
Turning friendships into thieves,
Once golden bonds now cold and bare,
Lost to silence, fading air.

They were the light when days felt dark,
Now echoes dim without a spark.
And in a heartbeat, like breath turned thin,
They leave, a ghost beneath your skin.

Oh, healer—know your scars are true,
For every heart, there's one for you.
Remember, too, in your gentle grace,
A healer's heart needs its own embrace.

Seek the warmth you give away,
Let soft hands press on you and stay.
The love you offer, let it return,
In embers kindling, let yourself burn.

For you are worthy, just as they,
Of care and light, of hope and day.
Dear healer's heart, find peace, be whole,
For even healers need a soul.

5. The Sharpest Silence

You said I was your closest friend,
A bond you swore would never end.
I held your fears, your sleepless nights,
But now you leave with bitter bites.

The words you spoke, they cut so deep,
A backstab strong, no tears to weep.
"You're not the one who used to care,"
Yet I was there, when no one would dare.

I listened while your world collapsed,
Each wound you bore, each scar relapsed.
Yet now you claim I've lost that ear,
As if my love could disappear.

You knew I stood alone, confined,
No other arms, no peace to find.
But still, you chose to twist the blade,
And left me drowning in the shade.

Those letters you once wrote with pride,
Now rot within, where truths collide.
Each word of thanks, each praise you gave,
Now buried deep, within my grave.

How cruel the shift from love to scorn,
A friendship turned, its fabric torn.
I trusted you, you let me fall,
Now silence echoes through it all.

I see your face in every line,
A haunting ghost of what was mine.
But ghosts can't hurt what's dead inside,
In ashes now, where love had died.

So here I stand, with scars unshown,
A heart once shared, now cold, alone.
Your voice may fade, but pain remains,
A silent storm in endless rains.

6. The Unseen Flame

I am the candle burning in the darkest room,
Silent and steadfast, chasing away the gloom.
Yet, they curse me for the single flicker,
Ignoring the wax I've shed, now thinner.

My hands, they built bridges from endless storms,
A labour of love, shaping sacred forms.
But one stone misplaced, a ripple they see,
And the ocean of effort dissolves silently.

I have been the anchor in tempest's wail,
The quiet force behind every sail.
Yet when the ship tilts in a single gust,
They bury my devotion beneath their mistrust.

Am I the shadow, unseen by the light?
A ghost of loyalty in their limited sight?
Or a tree that bends until it breaks,
For every unseen storm it bravely takes?

Call me selfish; I've no defense,
My sacrifices lie in quiet pretence.
For those who count faults on fragile scales,
Will never know the depth of untold tales.

I am the sun, rising to warm their days,
They curse the dusk, but not the blaze.
Let them speak, for I am still the flame,
Burning brightly, untouched by blame.

7. The Healer's Burden

They come to me with hearts undone,
With broken souls and battles spun.
I stitch their wounds, I mend their pain,
Yet walk alone in silent rain.
I am the light in darkest night,
The steady hand, the guiding sight.
I whisper hope where shadows grow,
Yet in my chest, the echoes flow.
Their sorrow seeps into my veins,
A silent weight, a ghostly chain.
I wear a smile, serene and true,
But sometimes, healers need one too.
Who soothes the hand that wipes the tears?
Who quiets all the hidden fears?
Who lifts the healer when they fall,
When their own storms begin to call?
The trees still sway when winds arise,
The sun still dims in cloudy skies.
Even the strongest rivers wane,
Even the bravest know of pain.
So when you see the healer's frown,
A weary soul weighed heavy down,
Offer a touch, a word, a light—
For even healers need respite.

For though we mend, though we renew,
Sometimes, a healer needs one too.

8. The Quiet Farewell

Once we danced in golden light,
Shared our dreams through endless night.
Laughter echoed, voices bright,
A bond that felt so true, so right.
But silence crept where words once grew,
Like autumn leaves in morning dew.
I reached for you, you slipped away,
A fading hue in skies of gray.
I overthink, retrace the past,
Where did we change? Why didn't we last?
You withdraw, a step, then two,
A bridge we built—now split in two.
No angry words, no bitter fight,
Just distance stretching out of sight.
A hollow space, a quiet ache,
A thread too thin, too worn to take.
But love that stays will find a way,
Through storms and nights and skies of gray.
If you still care, you'll turn around,
If not, I'll stand on solid ground.
Some friendships fade, some slip and go,
Not all departures loud will show.
So if you leave, I'll set you free,
No chains, no pleas—just memories.

9. Silent Sorrows

I wear a smile, bright and wide,
A perfect mask, a truth denied.
For when I speak, the echoes play,
Turning pain to jest and sway.
They laugh at wounds they cannot see,
A fleeting joke at the cost of me.
My sorrow shrinks beneath their gaze,
Drowned in careless, hollow praise.
If words betray, then let them fade,
I'll lock my grief in silent shade.
A quiet heart, a steady face,
No need for pity, no need for grace.
Yet silence sings its lonely tune,
A gentle ache beneath the moon.
Would someone hear if I let go?
Or would they laugh and never know?
But maybe strength is standing tall,
To speak the hurt, to risk the fall.
For even shadows need the light,
And silent hearts deserve the night.
So if I smile, just look inside,
Beyond the walls where fears reside.
Not every laugh is free of pain,
Not every silence hides in vain.

10. The Weight of Letting Go

I spoke in whispers, soft and true,
Hoping you'd see my heart's deep hue.
I held my pain in open hands,
Yet you just let it slip like sand.
I tried, I stayed, I bent, I broke,
But love should not be choked by smoke.
If understanding needs a plea,
Then maybe you were never free.
Some bridges burn, some fade in time,
Some words get lost between the lines.
And begging hearts to stay or see,
Is just a cage without a key.
So I step back, let silence grow,
For peace is found in letting go.
No more the weight, no more the ache,
No ties to mend, no past to wake.
Not all who leave are lost in vain,
Not all goodbyes are meant for pain.
Some doors must close, some ties unwind,
To heal, to breathe, to free the mind.
And though it stings, I walk away,
For love should never need to stay.

If hearts don't meet in common space,
Then distance is the kindest grace.

11. Shattered Bonds

They say the heart finds solace near,
In friends who wipe away each tear.
But where to go, where to mend,
When the wound was left by a friend?
Not by a lover's fleeting grace,
Not by a stranger's careless face,
But hands once warm, a voice once true,
Now turned as cold as morning dew.
The trust we built, the laughs we shared,
The silent vows that someone cared—
All shattered now, a hollow space,
A name I flinch at, time won't erase.
No hand to hold, no arms to stay,
Just echoes left in yesterday.
Where do I run, where do I hide,
When even memories take their side?
Perhaps the heart must learn to stand,
To find its peace with trembling hands.
Not every scar needs hands to heal,
Not every pain deserves appeal.
So, I will go where silence sings,
Where I can mend my broken wings.
And when they ask where I have been,
I'll say, **"I found my strength within."**

12. Silence Isn't Ego

They call it pride, they call it spite,
When I choose silence over fight.
But not all quiet comes from scorn,
Some wounds are best when left unworn.
I do not speak, I do not plead,
Not out of hate, not out of greed.
But when words fall on deafened ears,
Silence speaks what no one hears.
Not every pause is meant to hurt,
Not every stillness drips with dirt.
Sometimes, to step away is grace,
To leave behind a losing race.
I do not owe the world my pain,
Nor must I scream to make it plain.
If understanding needs a shout,
Then maybe it's not worth the doubt.
So judge me not for what I lack,
 For words unsaid I won't take back.
 For every quiet isn't pride,
 But peace found deep, with none to chide.

13. Empty Victory

In heated words, the past is thrown,
A debt unpaid, a love outgrown.
I stand, I speak, but all in vain,
For kindness now is weighed in pain.
They turn and ask with hollow pride,
"After all you did, who stood by your side?"
As if my worth, my heart, my time,
Were coins to count, a worthless dime.
I did not give to make them stay,
I did not love for debt to pay.
But now they twist what once was true,
And in their game, I seem to lose.
But did I lose, or did I see,
The truth they tried to hide from me?
For love that tallies, love that weighs,
Was never love—it was a phase.
So let them think they won this fight,
Let them stand tall in hollow light.
If keeping score is how they play,
Then losing them was my escape.

14. Missed Moments

You think I miss you in the rain,
When silence sings, when hearts feel drained?
No, not in sorrow, not in pain—
I miss you when life shines again.
When laughter spills, when skies turn bright,
When dreams take shape in golden light.
When victories bloom, when joy is near,
I look around—you're not here.
Not in the nights of endless grey,
But in the mornings washed in day.
Not when I weep, not when I fall,
But when I rise and wish to call.
You were the first I'd run to tell,
Each story shared, each triumph swelled.
Now echoes fill the space you left,
A happy heart, yet still bereft.
So don't believe I miss you low,
I miss you most when moments glow.
For loneliness can fade away,
But joy still aches when you can't stay.

15. Silent Echoes

The wind may howl, the branches creak,

Yet neither know the tale they speak.

A storm once stirred in skies untold,

Yet half-truths dance on lips so bold.

The river hums but does not see,

The roots that twist beneath the tree.

A fragment floats upon the tide,

But depths remain where truths still hide.

A lantern flickers in the mist,

Yet shadows stretch where lies persist.

A whispered word, a careless sigh,

Can twist the truth and let it die.

A mountain stands through endless time,

Yet none have scaled its highest climb.

And still they claim to know its height,

While staring up from borrowed light.

So hush, let silence be your grace,

Not every tale needs eager chase.

For echoes lie and winds deceive,

And half a story makes one grieve.

If words must rise, let wisdom guide,

Not fickle tongues nor hollow pride.

For those who speak yet do not see,

Are prisoners of their own decree.

16. A Leaf in the Wind

I was a star in a sky so wide,
Yet you cast your gaze to the fickle tide.
A candle waiting in patient glow,
Yet you chose the storm, let the fire go.
Like autumn leaves that twist and sway,
You held my name but threw it away.
A whisper lost in a crowded room,
Yet I still stayed, blind to my doom.
You played your game with careless hands,
Weaving me into shifting sands.
A fleeting thought, a passing face,
Never mine, just borrowed space.
But I am no echo, no waiting shore,
No open window, no half-closed door.
If you hesitate, then I step away,
For I am not a game to play.
A flower won't bloom where roots don't grow,
Nor chase the sun if shadows show.
So I walk away with steady feet,
A choice made strong, a soul complete.
For love is not a whispered plea,
But steady hands and certainty.
And those who treat your heart so light,
Should fade like stars in morning light.

17. The Anchor Within

I have wandered through the howling night,
Chased shadows lost in borrowed light.
Gave away my voice, my name, my fire,
Only to drown in their quiet desire.
I bent like branches in the wind,
Let every storm pull me within.
Tied my worth to fleeting hands,
To love that slipped like shifting sands.
But a river that forgets its course,
Is left to fate, to drift, to force.
And I have learned, through tears and dust,
That love means nothing without self-trust.
So now I stand, unchained, untamed,
No longer lost, no longer named—
By those who came and left me bare,
Who only stayed when it was fair.
I do not chase, I do not plead,
For I have found all that I need.
A heart that beats, a soul that stays,
An echo strong in silent days.
So let them leave, let bridges burn,
I will not twist, I will not turn.
For I don't care who walks away,
If I am here to stay.

18. The Road Through Ruin

I took a path of shattered stone,
A road not meant to walk alone.
Each step I took, a fractured choice,
A whispered doubt, a silenced voice.
I chased the stars, then lost my way,
Tripped on words I didn't say.
Built castles high on borrowed dreams,
Watched them fall in silent screams.
Yet in the wreckage, roots took hold,
In dust and ash, in stories old.
The bridges burned, the rivers strayed,
Yet here I stand—no more afraid.
For every wrong turn carved a guide,
A lesson buried deep inside.
Some doors must close, some ties must break,
For fate to shape the path we take.
So let me stumble, let me fall,
Let regret mean nothing at all.
For some mistakes, though dressed in pain,
Are maps that lead through fire and rain.
And now I see, through scars and time,
That every loss was truly mine—
Not as defeat, nor as despair,
But steps that led me to be there.

19. The Price of Silence

A door left open, a whispered plea,
A kindness stretched too carelessly.
I let them take, I let them stay,
Till I was lost in yesterday.
I bent like reeds in endless tide,
Let careless hands pull me inside.
I gave my time, I gave my trust,
Yet love returned in scattered dust.
A lesson learned in quiet pain—
That silence builds a binding chain.
For every time I let it slide,
I taught them it was justified.
A heart too patient, soft and kind,
Becomes a cage, leaves you confined.
The more you bear, the less they see,
Till all you are used debris.
But now I rise, my voice is clear,
No space for doubt, no room for fear.
For those who love will never need,
A lesson carved in silent bleed.
So be not quiet, be not meek,
Demand the love you dare to seek.
For how you bend is how they'll mold,
And what you take is what they'll hold.

20. The Eccedentesiast's Farewell

I wore a smile like a practiced art,
A painted mask, a shielded heart.
An eccedentesiast, bright and bold,
Hiding stories left untold.
I gave my light, my soul, my time,
Stood in shadows, made them shine.
A silent ghost in crowded halls,
Yet no one heard my quiet calls.
So, one day, I slipped away,
No words to beg, no need to stay.
Not out of spite, nor bitter rage,
But to step beyond a scripted stage.
For who was I, if not their need?
A thread unravelling, left to bleed.
But now I walk where I belong,
A rhythm set to my own song.
Never feel guilt for vanishing light,
The stars don't ask the sun for flight.
I needed me, more than they knew,
And in the quiet, I broke through.
So, if they ask, just let them miss—
For I was never made for this.

21. The Ghosts We Create

The night is quiet, the stars still gleam,
Yet shadows dance within my dream.
A voice unheard, a fate unknown,
A fear that chills me to the bone.
I see the storms before they rise,
Feel the tears in unshed cries.
The walls around me start to fall,
Yet nothing's touched them—nothing at all.
A battle waged inside my mind,
Of days undone, of paths confined.
Yet when the dawn paints gold anew,
I find the fear was never true.
We suffer more in thought than pain,
Bound by chains that aren't real chains.
A prison built from whispered doubt,
A door unlocked, yet never walked out.
So, hush, dear mind, the war is done,
The sky still holds the steady sun.
Let go, let breathe, let silence be,
Not every fear is destiny.
For life is kinder than we know,
If only we would let it show.